T0014434

Connecting the Dots

TWENTY-ONE DEVOTIONALS
BASED ON REAL-LIFE EXPERIENCES TO BETTER UNDERSTAND
KINGDOM PRINCIPLES

JASON O. YEARWOOD

CONNECTING THE DOTS
TWENTY-ONE DEVOTIONALS BASED ON REAL-LIFE EXPERIENCES
TO BETTER UNDERSTAND KINGDOM PRINCIPLES

iUniverse books may be ordered through booksellers or by contacting:

iUniverse
1663 Liberty Drive
Bloomington, IN 47403
www.iuniverse.com
844-349-9409

ISBN: 978-1-6632-2456-9 (sc)
ISBN: 978-1-6632-3150-5 (e)

Library of Congress Control Number: 2021922829

Print information available on the last page.

iUniverse rev. date: 11/24/2021

I dedicate this book to the Lord God, whose love for us has no depths. Through the death and resurrection of his son Jesus and the guidance of the Holy Spirit, we are presented with the opportunity to enjoy life, on earth and beyond, within his kingdom and under his governance.

To my lovely wife Jakita, thank you for your tangible and intangible contributions to this God-ordained work. I deeply appreciate your valuable support at every step of this journey, particularly your editing, guidance and recommendations. I love you dearly and I thank the Lord that He has blessed me with such an amazing wife, friend, confidant and companion.

To the two strong pillars in my life, my mother Cherylann and my late grandmother, Priscilla, tears of immense gratefulness stream down my face as I write this note of acknowledgement. Words cannot begin to express the indelible impact you both have had on my life. Considering the nature of this devotional, it is even clearer to me that God has used you both as critical tools over these years towards the fulfilment of this good work which he started. I love you both.

My father, Nigel, thank you for your support in all of my endeavours and for realising my talent to write at an early age, and thus encouraging me since then to release work. It has now come to pass.

My close friends and brothers, Wilando and Ezron, thank you for your encouragement to collate all these devotionals into a book. Your continued encouragement is greatly appreciated.

To each of the endorsers and my church family at The People's Cathedral in Bridgetown Barbados, thank you for your love, ministry and tutelage. May the Lord continue to use each of you as an instrument of change.

To Abigail Ali, thank you for capturing the vision of this kingdom project and designing a wonderful cover design concept.

I wish to thank the team at iUniverse for their professional skill in making this work a reality for sharing with the world.

Finally, and with a grateful heart, I thank the Lord my God through whom all things remain possible.

In *Connecting the Dots*, Jason Yearwood uses sound biblical principles to present a holistic message of the kingdom of God. This, accompanied by practical, relevant and relatable illustrations, has resulted in a mature yet contemporary book that will inspire Christians and unbelievers alike in any demographic. A refreshing devotional, this book not only causes the reader to engage in sober self-examination but to also rejoice in the Lord Jesus Christ, who is wonderfully represented on every page.

Reverend Jewell Callender
Senior Pastor, The Peoples Cathedral
Barbados

A thoughtful and encouraging daily walk with God. Three weeks of material to energize your personal devotional times.

Bishop Dr Gerald Seale
Former Presiding Bishop
Pentecostal Assemblies of the West Indies (PAWI), Barbados District

I have read a number of devotionals over the years and have received many blessings and encouragement along the way. Having read *Connecting the Dots*, I am thrilled at the nuggets that God has given to Jason to impact us in and for the kingdom. As you draw down from the truths from this devotional, your life will be thoroughly enriched.

Reverend Edwin Bullen
Senior Pastor, Christ Is the Answer Family Church, Barbados

While his feet are firmly planted on earth, Jason O. Yearwood, as a citizen of God's kingdom and with a kingdom mindset, is experiencing heaven on earth. *Connecting the Dots* is a compilation of personal experiences which illuminate principles of God's kingdom in Mr. Yearwood's life. Through the lessons of each encounter, God's provision in the face of life's realities taught Jason Yearwood how citizens of God's kingdom can practically live under God's government. I am delighted to endorse this timely kingdom witness in the hope that it would strengthen the kingdom focus of believers in our present-day world system and invite nonbelievers to accept Christ and enter His everlasting kingdom.

Pastor Dennis E White
Ontario, Canada

Is your kingdom citizenship secured? Well, here is your opportunity to apply.

Connecting the Dots: Twenty-One Devotionals written by Jason O. Yearwood is an intriguing and inspirational guide that compels its readers to start the application process *now*.

This book reveals the author's heart as he meticulously shares his personal, real-life experiences while echoing the sound doctrine of an unshakeable Christian kingdom lifestyle. His insightful words of encouragement and biblical references are timely as we search for answers to help us through the present covid-19 pandemic chaos. The voice of the author is resonant and his words are spiritually uplifting and thought-provoking. After each of his personal reveals, you will be ushered into God's amazing presence to reflect on your own journey as you navigate throughout your life's challenges. As you read, may you be empowered to ask for God's divine help and in so doing be engaged in a flowing stream of continuous praise.

As I continue to savour this gourmet meal, I am propelled to 'self-audit' and connect the dots, dial a few friends, and initiate a virtual discussion with the question: Are your dots connected? I did.

This is a *must* read.

Rev M Burton, BA, BEd, MA
Community Service Chaplain
The International Association of Community Service Chaplains
Ontario, Canada

CONTENTS

Introduction..xiii

Section 1 – Laying the Foundation 1

   Day 1 – The 'New Normal' Has Already Come 3

   Day 2 – Commit: Carry into Deliberate Action.........................6

   Day 3 – It's Time to Come Clean...9

   Day 4 – Trust in Jesus and He Will Show You 11

   Day 5 – No Nitpicking 14

   Day 6 – Catchphrases... 16

   Day 7 – Russian Roulette 19

Section 2 – Learning the Pattern 23

   Day 8 – Focusing on What Matters I–Reality Check...............25

   Day 9 – Focusing on What Matters II–Knowledge is Power.....27

   Day 10 – Focusing on What Matters III–Kingdom Focus........30

   Day 11 – Pillow Talk..33

   Day 12 – Trust: God versus Man 36

   Day 13 – The Importance of Self-Auditing 39

   Day 14 – Critical Thinking and Decision Making 42

Section 3 — Taking Shape **45**

    Day 15 — Putting it into Practice 47

    Day 16 — One of the Greatest 49

    Day 17 — Making Wealth Common 52

    Day 18 — Gratitude is a Must 55

    Day 19 — Kick Doubt to the Kerb and Believe! 58

    Day 20 — The Unconventional Lifestyle 61

    Day 21 — Family Ties 64

Conclusion: The Big Picture 67

INTRODUCTION

Developing Strategy

For approximately two decades, my mother worked in a department store. Items such as furniture, household appliances, televisions, VCRs and DVDs (I'm a '90s kid), bicycles, musical instruments, garden tools, and much more were sold at this once-historic, now rebranded company. I spent many a day at her branch location, exploring what to the 6- and 7-year-old me were 'new discoveries,' and had first-hand experience observing how the company operated and conducted business with customers seeking to make a purchase.

In later years, when I was introduced to the concept of hire purchase (an arrangement for buying expensive consumer goods) in my elementary mathematics class, I was able to recall the interactions I saw at my mother's workplace. This earlier life experience greatly contributed to my understanding of this mathematical concept.

As I have grown in my spiritual walk, I have become more aware of and sensitive to the way God uses life experiences and encounters to bring biblical principles and kingdom concepts to life. Every encounter and experience serves a purpose of teaching us something of God's immeasurable love, his direction for our lives, and His sovereign nature. The bigger picture of what God wants to teach us unfolds bit by bit with every new life experience. In this way, if life and its seasons were to be thought of as an unfinished connect-the-dot puzzle, each experience would be a dot that progressively leads to the bigger picture.

Of course, a critical component of this is to spend time reading the word of God. For many of us, this may be challenging. It is my prayer, therefore, that through this devotional series, the message of Christ, his gift of salvation, and the practicality of His teachings on kingdom living may be well received. Through connecting the dots of everyday life to our spiritual walk, we can surely make the application of kingdom principles in our lives a reality!

Scripture Verse

'The LORD says, "I will guide you along the best pathway for your life. I will advise you and watch over you.' (Psalm 32:8).

As we embark on this twenty-one day journey together, I encourage you to set aside at least ten minutes to unplug after each daily devotional. Allow for time to meditate and internalise the lessons of the kingdom that God illuminates in each devotional. According to your preference, grab a journal to pen some thoughts or just pause and have a true heart to heart with God.

Let's get started together.

Section One

LAYING THE FOUNDATION

And who can win this battle against the world? Only
those who believe that Jesus is the Son of God.
—1 John 5:5

DAY 1

The 'New Normal' Has Already Come

For the first half of 2020, the entire world grappled with the impacts of the outbreak of the novel coronavirus, COVID 19, which infected millions of persons across the globe. The impact of this highly infectious virus, of which the elderly and ailing were the most disadvantaged, spread much beyond its negative effects on health. Every facet of human life, to which we had grown accustomed in our respective global communities, was influenced in some way. So unprecedented was its level of interruption that the phrase 'new normal' had been used to describe what life will look like in the aftermath of the crisis.

Day after day, television and other media offered information detailing how world governments and global business organizations, including manufacturing, technological, and service sectors, travel and tourism entities, and sports organizations, could take steps together concerning the future operations of critical sectors. Specific focus was made on the implementation of policies and new social practices to safeguard the health of so-called frontline workers, and the wider public, against contracting COVID-19.

Simply put, our lives were disrupted in a major and undeniable way.

For many, the outbreak of COVID-19 was the first time witnessing global change at such magnitude. However, more than two thousand years ago, a series of events took place bigger than any pandemic or noted occurrence the world has ever seen. These events changed the course of human life on earth and in eternity.

That event was the birth, death, and resurrection of Jesus Christ, the son of God, the single most norm-disrupting, life-changing, future-impacting occurrence since God uttered creation into existence. Jesus was sent by God the father as his extension of grace, so that through him, those who believe and accept him may be reconciled to the kingdom of God and have everlasting life.

When Adam sinned in the garden of Eden, we lost our connection with our heavenly father. Through the coming of Jesus Christ, his death, and his resurrection, we can once again be put in right standing with God. We have been given the blueprint and access that we need to lead victorious lives until we are welcomed home in glory.

The new normal is already here. Let us be encouraged to take hold of it.

Scripture Verse

'This means that anyone who belongs to Christ has become a new person. The old life is gone; a new life has begun!' (2 Corinthians 5:17).

Reflection

If after reading this devotional and you are moved to embrace the 'new normal' that is available through Christ Jesus, simply say this prayer and believe in your heart:

Dear Lord, I come to you today acknowledging that I am a sinner. Amidst all that has transpired in my life, I ask that you forgive me of my sins and wash me clean by the blood of Jesus. I believe that you sent Jesus to die on the cross for my sins and through his resurrection, I am reconnected to your kingdom and am in right standing with you. I commit this day to live for you, with all my heart, soul and mind and ask that through your Holy Spirit, you guide me along the path of righteousness. These things I pray in the mighty name of Jesus Christ, amen.

Welcome to the family of the kingdom of God.

DAY 2

Commit: Carry into Deliberate Action

I love food. Anyone who knows me well can validate this. Fried chicken, grilled fish, barbecue delights such as burgers, chicken, and ribs, french fries, and mac 'n' cheese are some of my favourite dishes. In my younger days, I overindulged. I always looked forward to Friday nights when the guys and I got together to visit a popular fast food spot and get our orders up-sized. In fact, I like food so much that when I first introduced my girlfriend (now wife) to my now-deceased grandmother, she told her, 'I hope you know how to cook because he too loves his belly.'

Not surprisingly, my love for food and my cavalier way of eating came at some costs, one of them having to wear a size thirty-eight waist at age 21. This wasn't a good path to be on, and one could only surmise the likely end results a continuation on this path would cause, if a swift change was not enacted.

So in 2013, I committed to maintaining a healthier lifestyle. I chose healthier meal options, reduced my portion sizes, and embarked on a consistent exercise routine, all towards the goal of being healthy. Within three months, I lost thirty pounds. I felt great, looked greater, and became even more self-confident, knowing the changes I made were for my future benefit.

If we are honest with ourselves, we as humans are often drawn to worldly vices, such as fornication, alcoholism, abuse of illegal drugs, lying, stealing, taking advantage of others, all of which cause us to lead lives that are contrary to what God expects of us. Just like maintaining a poor diet can possibly lead to excessive weight gain and other health complications, to engage in worldly vices is to sin against God and continuing down this path will lead to spiritual destruction, 'for the wages of sin is death' (Romans 6:23).

However, that same verse goes on to say, 'but the free gift of God is eternal life through Christ Jesus our Lord.'

To receive this gift, all we have to do is *commit*: take deliberate action in accepting Jesus Christ in our hearts, and seek daily to live for him. As someone who has taken that step and strives to live daily for him, I can tell you that just like the benefits of losing weight are tremendous, committing to a life in Christ is equally rewarding, with benefits to be enjoyed here on earth and in the life to come.

I encourage us all to take that step and commit to Christ today. God has already taken deliberate action in giving us the gift of salvation through Jesus Christ.

If God, the Almighty, all-knowing, and all-powerful being that He is has committed to us, we too can certainly commit to Him.

Scripture Verse

'For this is how God loved the world; He gave his one and only Son, so that everyone who believes in him will not perish but have eternal life' (John 3:16).

Reflection

What are some areas in your life that you need to deliberately commit to in order to see the improvements you desire? Write down what are the possible steps you need to take to achieve this improvement and strive daily to fulfil them.

DAY 3

It's Time to Come Clean

I once watched a television show called *Hoarding: Buried Alive*. One particular episode featured a lady who had a clean and tidy home on the surface, but she had a deep and troubled history of hoarding. For years she just collected, collected, and collected. She collected so much that not only did she have a full basement, but what were once the rooms of her now adult children were filled to capacity. Additionally, she rented two storage lockers and a nine thousand square-foot commercial space, all to satisfy her hoarding tendencies.

To compound this situation, her husband was growing increasingly upset with her habit, to the extent that it brought their marriage to a crossroads. To make matters worse, he wasn't even aware of the second storage unit or the commercial space she rented in the city.

In an effort to break free from this addiction, she sought professional help from a clinical psychologist, who told her the first step in overcoming her addiction is to be honest and come clean to her husband and inform him of the other hoarding locations.

Spiritually speaking, we all have found ourselves in hoarding situations. We've been through many struggles or have bad habits that we just haven't been able to break free from, but which we drag with us to each stage of our lives. This in turn hinders us from accepting the gift of salvation which God the father extends to us through Jesus Christ. We often feel ashamed to come clean and lay out before the Lord the baggage we carry and grapple with. We think that we have to clean this and that up before we present ourselves to him.

Brothers and sisters, Jesus Christ is not deterred by our faults or bad habits. Rather, his desire is to meet us where we are, and he delights to be our source of strength in times of weakness. When we allow him to do this and accept him into our lives, he will set us free from the bondage that holds us back from a life of peace and rest in him.

Let us come clean and be set free.

Scripture Verse

'Come to me, all you who are weary and carry heavy burdens, and I will give you rest. Take my yoke upon you. Let me teach you, because I am humble and gentle at heart, and you will find rest for your souls. For my yoke is easy to bear, and the burden I give you is light' (Matthew 11:28–30).

Reflection

What bad habits or tendencies have you been in denial about or kept secret? When you have identified them, come clean before the Lord in prayer asking for His strength and guidance to overcome them.

DAY 4

Trust in Jesus and He Will Show You

Whilst listening to an episode of one of my favourite sports podcasts, the topic of the Dallas Cowboys signing Aldon Smith for the 2020–2021 NFL season was being discussed. The number seven overall pick in the 2011 NFL draft, Smith's first three seasons as a defensive outside line-backer were nothing but extraordinary, recording a total of forty-two sacks. This was ranked as the third most sacks by any player in their first three seasons throughout the history of the NFL.

Sadly, Smith's career began to be derailed by a series of off-the-field incidents which included multiple DUI charges, violations of the NFL's substance abuse and personal conduct policies, and a hit and run incident. After enduring a number of suspensions handed down by the league's head office, he was subsequently suspended for the entire 2015 season after nine games and had not played in the league since.

In 2020, however, after completing intervention programs mainly targeting his problems with substance abuse, Smith was reported as clean and sober and was thereafter signed by the Cowboys pending reinstatement by the NFL. Despite this, many analysts, though in support of him receiving a second opportunity, aired their trepidations of Smith and his potential level of production, considering his almost five-year absence from the league.

On the podcast mentioned above, one analyst described his trepidations of Smith to match his production in his formative years this way: 'I can't trust him. I am glad that he has received a second opportunity and I hope he does well, but I can't trust him to produce like before. You know, God says trust me and I'll show you, but humans say show me and then I'll trust you ... and I am a human.'

As humans, we are highly evidence-based. We usually like to see before we believe. This oftentimes is a major barrier for many of us as we think that to gain the trust of others, we have to be just right or perfect before we may gain their approval.

However, thank God for Jesus! He welcomes us as we are, regardless of whatever chequered past we may have.

Not only does he welcome us, he invites us to trust him, knowing that he is the one who may fulfil our desire to change.

So not only may we freely come, but we have the assurance of knowing that he will help us change, so we don't have to do it on our own.

Scripture Verse

'Trust in the Lord with all your heart; do not depend on your own understanding. Seek his will in all you do, and he will show you which path to take' (Proverbs 3:5-6).

Reflection

A key component of living a victorious life in Christ is to understand that it is through him that we are changed and not by our own might. Trust Jesus to be your agent of change.

DAY 5

No Nitpicking

E ver have the feeling that for some people, your best just isn't enough? In the modern world, satisfying pre-set standards seems to be everything, especially within the professional arena.

I once watched a wedding cake competition on the Food Network where top-rated contestants vied for the title of wedding cake champion and bragging rights for being the top wedding cake creator in the United States.

On one challenge, the chefs were required to create a wedding cake topper based on a beach wedding theme. One contestant did such a tremendous job that the first two judges sang her praises on the taste, design, and overall composition of the piece. The third judge also echoed the sentiments of his counterparts but then proceeded to say that he had a problem with the inclusion of rose petals, as it didn't go hand in hand with a beach wedding theme.

Puzzled face! Umm ... aren't rose petals and flowers a common feature at weddings regardless of location? Plus, the petals weren't even the focal point of the presentation. Talk about nitpicking.

After accepting Jesus into our hearts and receiving the gift of salvation, the kingdom of God requires us to live up to the righteous standards as outlined by God the father in the bible and later taught and exhibited by Jesus when he walked the earth.

However, God already knows that as we aim to meet these standards, we will at some point stumble and may fall. For as Isaiah 64:6 says, "We are all infected and impure with sin. When we display our righteous deeds, they are nothing but filthy rags. Like autumn leaves, we wither and fall, and our sins sweeps us away like the wind.

Here's the difference. At the times when we veer off path along our quest towards righteousness, rather than nitpicking and highlighting our faults, God is there to pick us up and set us back on the right course.

Be confident in knowing that we serve a loving Creator who walks with us every step of the way and like the Good Shepherd that he is, he will never leave us nor forsake us.

Scripture Verse

'So now there is no condemnation for those who belong to Christ Jesus' (Romans 8:1).

Reflection

Take a moment to think about instances when you may have fallen short and it then became a focal point for other people. Lay those moments and associated feelings at the feet of God. As you do this, also ask Him to help you improve in those areas.

DAY 6

Catchphrases

Growing up, I was heavily entertained by the WWF (now the WWE). Remember, I'm a '90s kid! I recall days in elementary school where my friends and I recounted the events of the latest episodes and had strong debates about who our favourite wrestlers were and who was the best of them all.

One component I thoroughly enjoyed was hearing the catchphrases of the popular wrestlers. Back then, Stone Cold Steve Austin and The Rock were crowd favourites. They both were electrifying in their characters, moves, and speech. They knew how to get the crowd on their feet. Catchphrases such as 'And that's the bottom line because Stone Cold said so!' and 'If ya smell ... what The Rock ... is ... cooking!' really ignited a feeling of excitement across the worldwide wrestling community.

Another prominent and championship-decorated wrestler who had a famous catchphrase is Ric Flair. His went something like this: 'I'm Ric Flair! The stylin', profilin', limousine riding, jet flying, kiss-stealing, wheelin' and dealin' son of a gun', which was followed by his iconic rallying cry: 'Wooooooooooo!' This really got the audience pumped. Even to this day, when he makes a guest appearance, the crowd is just abuzz with energy.

As I got older, I came into the knowledge and understanding that wrestling is all scripted, and over time, I gradually drifted away from a deep enjoyment of this form of entertainment. I will admit I still enjoy seeing the high-flying and super-strength acts of the athletes performing (my wife absolutely abhors it), so I may watch the highlight recap of recent episodes from time to time.

One day though, I got to thinking. Considering the colourful and descriptive catchphrases of these athletes, what would a catchphrase that represents Jesus be like? I'm thinking that it would go something like this: 'I am the all-powerful, demon-chasing, stronghold breaking, ever-healing, need-providing, grace-abounding, never-forsaking, life-giving, all-loving, King of kings and Lord of lords, the Messiah of the world ... Jesus Christ!' (Talk about goose bumps!) Now that is a catchphrase that would get the adrenaline pumping.

The major difference is, unlike the WWE, nothing about Jesus is scripted. He's actually all of the above and much, much more.

Scripture Verse

'I am the Alpha and the Omega—the beginning and the end,' says the Lord God. 'I am the one who is, who always was, and who is still to come—the Almighty One' (Revelation 1:8).

Reflection

If you had to write a catchphrase for Jesus and what he means to you, what would it be? Write it down.

DAY 7

Russian Roulette

By its basic definition, Russian roulette is 'an act of bravado consisting of spinning the cylinder of a revolver loaded with one cartridge, pointing the muzzle at one's own head, and pulling the trigger.' (Merriam-Webster Dictionary)

Considering its definition and the serious and also fatal implications that can result, the phrase is also used to describe an activity that is potentially dangerous.

Over the years of relationship with my wife, including the early dating stages, we have enjoyed moments of play, pranks, and jokes with each other. On one occasion, we were up to our usual shenanigans. She was tidying the house and I was assisting (although she would probably say I was being more of a nuisance). She was about to return the broom and dustpan to the storage room when she cheekily hit me before proceeding to run. Naturally, she, thinking that I was chasing her (which I wasn't) ran and closed the door of the storage room, shutting herself in.

Seeing what she did, I decided why not play along? The idea came to me to push against the door with my hands so that when she sought to come out, she would be trapped. I thought it was a brilliant plan and followed through. A few moments passed ... no sound, no struggle. What was she doing in there?

In my curiosity, I pulled the door open just enough to get a peek inside but not enough to let her escape. In her haste and playful excitement, she darted her hand forward as soon as the door cracked opened, which she was waiting to do while she remained still. I was not aware of her plan. Unfortunately, I was a bit too fast in counteracting her offense and ended up slamming the door on her pinkie finger. Ouch!

What was previously laughter turned to shrieks of pain with the accompanying cries of, '*Oww! My finger, my finger, my finger!*'

I released the door and sought immediately to comfort her. Thankfully, there were no major injuries. The finger was bloodshot, swollen, and sore for a couple days, but has healed well thanks to God and some home remedies.

The reality is, things could have turned out very differently. We could not have known that a simple moment of childlike play would have resulted in personal injury.

Yet there are other instances when we are fully aware of what the possible outcome will be. But we are sometimes so engulfed by the good feelings within those moments that we don't consider that we are playing a very dangerous game—with our souls! Living a life outside salvation is like playing Russian Roulette. It's all fun and games until you have to face the consequences. No one knows when their number will be called, and as such, we shouldn't leave such a critical decision to a later stage in life such as the common, 'when I get older' or 'after one last hurrah.'

When God created earth, everything was perfect until man committed an act of disobedience which allowed sin to separate us from God and His righteousness (see Genesis 3). Thankfully, God gave us his ultimate home remedy by sending his only begotten Son, Jesus, to die the death appointed to us. Through this, we have the opportunity now to be reconciled to the kingdom (see John 3:16).

Now is the time to make the right decision in accepting God's gift of salvation. The time we have on earth is limited and no one knows when their time will expire. What is certain though is that, "...just as each person is destined to die once and after that comes judgment," (Hebrews 9:27).

Dear friends, we have a choice to make. Will we lead lives where we willingly engage in sin with its only result being death? Or will we accept God's free gift of salvation and have eternal life?

Scripture Verse

'For the wages of sin is death, but the free gift of God is eternal life through Christ Jesus our Lord' (Romans 6:23).

Reflection

As you reflect upon this devotional, think about persons you know who are currently playing Russian Roulette with their life. Take a moment now to pray for them to accept Christ Jesus into their heart once and for all. Also, don't forget to share the gospel at every opportunity.

Section Two

LEARNING THE PATTERN

So faith comes from hearing, that is, hearing
the Good News about Christ.
—Romans 10:17

Focusing on What Matters
I—Reality Check

The 2020 global Covid-19 outbreak and its perilous impacts drew comparisons to the Great Depression of the 1930s. Experts across many fields dubbed it as the Great Lockdown, since everyone was encouraged to *#staysafe and #stayhome*.

One lesson that many of us have learnt is that there is more to life than the material and finite things that we seek, such as wealth, property, or educational accolades. The pursuit of these sometimes makes life seem like an endless cycle. It feels like we're hamsters endlessly running on a wheel. We expend vast amounts of resources trying to reach what we define as life achievements but realize with each one under our belt, there is yet much more ground to cover.

Many of us are determined to cover that ground and do what it takes to achieve our goals as planned. However, that process can leave us feeling so battered, bruised and fatigued that by the time we reach those goals, we are in no state to thoroughly enjoy them. To compound this in some cases, one needs to invest further resources to protect what assets they have obtained. There's also the reality that these material possessions are fleeting and can be lost in the blink of an eye.

In Matthew 6, Jesus encourages us to 'do not lay up for yourselves treasures on earth, where moth and rust destroy and where thieves break in and steal; but lay up for yourselves treasures in heaven, where neither moth nor rust destroys and where thieves do not break in and steal. (vs 19–20). Jesus also outlines that we need not 'worry about what we shall eat, or what we shall drink, or what we shall wear' (31), 'for our heavenly Father already knows all your needs' (32). Rather, our focus should be to 'seek the kingdom of God above all else, and live righteously, and He will give you everything you need.' (33).

Today, may our focus be zeroed in not on the pressures and ideologies of this world, but rather on the realities of God and His kingdom. This is what truly matters.

Scripture Verse

'That is why I tell you not to worry about everyday life—whether you have enough food and drink, or enough clothes to wear. Isn't life more than food, and your body more than clothing?' (Matthew 6:25).

Reflection

What do you think are some of the concepts and ideologies of this world that keep you distracted from the realities of the kingdom of God and how it operates? Take time daily to explore God's word with the help of the Holy Spirit, to understand more about the system of God's kingdom and how it operates.

DAY 9

Focusing on What Matters II–Knowledge is Power

In high school, I had a tough time with my Spanish classes. I wasn't failing, but I certainly wasn't at the top of the class. With an important series of exams approaching, I was just hoping to escape with a passing grade. One day, a classmate suggested I consider joining private Spanish lessons that he was attending. I enrolled, which turned out to be an excellent decision.

There, I was exposed to a wealth of knowledge that made reading, speaking, and listening to the language much easier. There was a major focus on learning idiomatic expressions which brought much life to the language. One such expression was *saber es poder,* which means knowledge is power. This phrase truly sums up my overall experience with this private class. Having obtained a wealth of knowledge, I was empowered to do extremely well on my Spanish exam. I moved from a barely passing grade to attaining one with distinction!

Drawing a parallel to one's spiritual walk, a key component of growth and development as a kingdom citizen is learning. This will not only benefit us personally but will also be to the benefit of those we come into contact with.

To do this, one must seek knowledge from the Bible. In it, God has highlighted the many ways in which we may

- build and improve our character;
- exercise discipline and self-control;
- foster better relationships;
- conduct good business practices; and
- be the best keeper we can be of our brothers and sisters.

To focus on what matters, we must have a knowledge of what exactly we need to do.

Through reading the Word, we can attain the knowledge of Christ. By implementing his teachings, we will be equipped and empowered to lead victorious lives.

Scripture Verse

'All Scripture is inspired by God and is useful to teach us what is true and to make us realize what is wrong in our lives. It corrects us when we are wrong and teaches us to do what is right. God uses it to prepare and equip his people to do every good work.' (2 Timothy 3:16–17).

Reflection

Starting and maintaining a regular bible-reading routine may be difficult for many. If you fall into this category, commit to reading at least one chapter a day starting with the Old Testament. With the help of the Holy Spirit, your knowledge of the kingdom and the person of God will surely be deepened. I can testify to this.

✦

DAY 10

Focusing on What Matters
III–Kingdom Focus

As part of my tenure at university whilst reading for my bachelor's degree, I had the opportunity to study abroad for two years in the Bahamas. Whilst there, I was fortunate to attend Bahamas Faith Ministries, which at the time was led by founder, evangelist, renowned author, speaker, and leadership consultant, the late Dr Myles Munroe.

My very first visit to the church came when Dr Myles was in the process of launching the theme of the year, which centred around kingdom citizenship. Over the ensuing weeks, Dr Myles, through careful analysis of the scriptures, specifically the recorded words of Jesus in the four gospels, taught on what it means to be a kingdom citizen and understanding God's country, meaning heaven. How God governs, cares for his people, the laws of the country, the way citizens are expected to live, and other concepts were all explored.

This experience was indeed an eye opener. From all the lessons learnt throughout that series, one general theme stood out to me: the kingdom of God is a real place, with a real system of government, a real economy, and a real society, similar to what we witness in our earthly reality.

The clarity of this brought further understanding to many of the teachings and individual experiences where God showed himself to me throughout my life. It connected the dots and continues to do so.

The bottom line is this: a foundational element of living as kingdom citizens here on earth is to understand that God's kingdom and the principles that operate within it are real. This goes beyond the on-the-surface belief of 'God exists.'

When Jesus taught the disciples to pray via what we know today as the Lord's prayer, He confirmed this reality when he stated: 'Our Father, who art in heaven, hallowed be thy name. Thy will be done on earth as it is in heaven.' In other words, Jesus was asking the Father to do on earth what is already done in the real society—that is, the kingdom of heaven.

To safely navigate this harsh world, we ought to embrace the reality of the country of heaven.

This will make facing and traversing the challenges of this world easier. As kingdom citizens, understanding our home country and living in accordance with its system of governance assures us that we have all we need to live successful lives during our time on earth.

Jason O. Yearwood

Scripture Verse

'Abraham was confidently looking forward to a city with eternal foundations, a city designed and built by God' (Hebrews 11:10).

Reflection

In this difficult world, how can you strive daily to live and operate with a kingdom mindset?

DAY 11

Pillow Talk

Sometimes on weekends and when time permits, my wife and I just have a conversation. (Side note: moments of discussion and conversation are great ways to maintain healthy relationships.) We cover many topics, but they predominantly involve God and living a Christian life.

On one occasion we spoke about the Bible, noting all the discussions that this world-renowned best-seller evokes. We have both come across people who have varied opinions on the Bible. Some say that information has been removed, others say it's contradictory, whilst others say that it's just a storybook. I'll be the first to admit that growing up, I never read my Bible. I found it difficult to read and understand.

However, when I was a teenager, a visiting evangelist to my local assembly gave a challenge in his message to read the Bible from cover to cover. I decided to take up the challenge and gave it a try. This was one of the best decisions I have ever made. Since then, I have read it cover to cover four times, and each time I learn something new!

So what was the change that occurred, causing me to move from not reading the Bible to reading it four times with understanding? God's revelation. Each time before I read, I ask Him to open my eyes and heart to receive the truth of His word and to understand His teachings.

From my readings within the word, I have learnt that understanding God's teachings and character, based on His revelation, is not unique to me:

- Second Timothy 3:16 speaks about scripture being written under the inspiration of God.
- Second Peter 1:21 speaks to the fact that 'those prophets were moved by the Holy Spirit, and they spoke from God.'
- In Matthew 16:13-20, Jesus asked his disciples who people say he is. After they gave the varied opinions of people, Jesus asked them who do they say Jesus is. Simon Peter responded, 'You are the Messiah, the Son of the living God.' Jesus replied, 'You are blessed, Simon of John, because my Father in heaven has revealed this you. You did not learn this from any human being.'

From the above examples, there is one common denominator. In each circumstance, reference is made to people either being inspired by or coming to knowledge through revelation from God.

Therefore, if scripture is inspired by God, and prophecy is spoken by God through human prophets, and Jesus confirmed that it was God that revealed knowledge to Simon Peter, then it can only be concluded that God is the only one we should rely on to guide us through the reading of His word.

Haven't we always been taught to gather our information straight from the horse's mouth?

Let us today ask God for His guidance, wisdom, and understanding as we read his word.

Scripture Verse

'For the Lord grants wisdom! From his mouth comes knowledge and understanding' (Proverbs 2:6).

Reflection

On each occasion that you set out to read the bible, ask the Lord to reveal the truth of his word to you.

Trust: God versus Man

I was enjoying another culinary competition show on the Food Network called Top Chef Canada. (Yes, I am a foodie in many respects.) In this series, twelve of the top chefs from across the country's provinces vie for the title of Top Chef Canada, along with other lucrative prizes.

As the competition progressed closer to the final round, eight participants remained to compete in a segment called Restaurant Wars. There were two groups of four, and each group was tasked with bringing a restaurant concept to life, from building a menu, to preparing and serving a three-course meal to the visiting diners and resident judges. Each team member was responsible for a specific part of the meal to allow for individual judging along with the team score.

Aligning with the segment's requirement for a full dinner service experience, each group had to appoint a team member to manage front-of-the-house operations. This responsibility included greeting and seating guests, directing the service team, and supervising the dining room floor. However, before these duties could be attended to by the appointed chefs, they had to prepare their competition dish first! Once prepped, they would then rely on their teammates in the kitchen to finish, plate, and present the meal.

Having settled into one team's restaurant, the judges weren't too impressed with the appetizer or main course. Noticing the judges' disappointment, the chef with front-of-the-house responsibilities, who had prepped the team's desserts, decided to go into the kitchen to ensure that her teammates completed and plated her desserts to set her up for success. Although she overheard the judges' comments of displeasure regarding her teammates' dishes, she refused to share this information with them, despite being asked. She did this because she knew that in the end, each chef would be judged by their individual meal regardless of it being a team competition.

When the scores were in, the aforementioned team lost, and two of its members were facing elimination. At the elimination table, the judges openly expressed their disappointment with the overall dining experience but singled out the dessert dish by the front-of-the-house manager as the best dish not only of the losing team, but overall. She therefore was exempted from elimination.

If she had not noticed the disappointment of the judges and thereafter sought to ensure that her plate was well done, would she have been saved to continue in the next round? Did she throw her team under the bus by going into self-survival mode, rather than trusting her teammates to assemble a great dessert plate? Should she have alerted the team about her observations and sought to come up with an idea to make amends for the benefit of the entire team?

This got me thinking. How many times do we put our trust in fellow man, only to be disappointed in the end, because those we trusted looked out for themselves at our expense? I've come to learn that putting our trust and hope in man goes against the cautioning of the Bible and often leads to a negative end.

Jason O. Yearwood

With God, we will never have this problem. He always has our best interest at heart, and through his love we have peace in knowing that in him, we will always be victorious.

Trusting man is a risk, but trusting God always pays dividends!

Scripture Verses

'Oh, the joys of those who trust the Lord, who have no confidence in the proud or in those who worship idols' (Psalm 40:4).

'You will keep in perfect peace all who trust you, all whose thoughts are fixed on you! Trust in the Lord always, for the Lord God is the eternal Rock' (Isaiah 26:3–4).

Reflection

What areas in your life do you trust man or man-made systems instead of trusting God?

DAY 13

The Importance of Self-Auditing

The Merriam-Webster Dictionary defines auditing as 'a formal examination of an organization's or individual's accounts or financial situation.' This term is used mainly within the financial and business sectors, but for the purposes of this devotional, let's look at it on the level of the individual.

As individuals, we all desire improvement in our lives. To move towards these improvements, we must take an "audit" of our current circumstances or assess where we are at and what steps we need to take towards the outcome.

Here are a few examples of self-audits that I have undertaken in my personal life:

- Educational—pinpointing the sacrifices and changes I needed to make during my tenure at university towards attaining first class honours.
- Financial—developing discipline in saving from each salary towards the goal of building wealth.
- Physical—making the decision to lose weight in 2013 with the goal of leading and maintaining a healthier, active lifestyle.

Drawing a parallel to our spiritual walk, taking self-audits as kingdom citizens is of vital importance. It is critical that we take an audit of our walk with the Lord, but more specifically, an audit of how we represent him in our homes, community networks, and social lives.

Here are a few questions that we as Christians need to ask ourselves during periods of spiritual self-auditing:

- Do I properly represent Christ?
- Am I known by the fruits of the Holy Spirit?
- Do I speak life and love, or do I pull down and castigate?
- Do I practise the act of forgiving others when wronged?
- Am I teachable, knowing when to admit my faults and listen to sound and constructive criticism?
- If those close to me were asked to comment on the way that I live as a kingdom citizen, what would they say?

A key component of self-development as a Christian is to know how to take a proper and honest audit of our spiritual walk and progress, with respect to how we are aligning with what God expects of us.

Doing this with the Lord's guidance will help us improve in areas of weakness, strengthening our message of salvation to a lost world. As the saying goes, 'The only Jesus that people see, is the Jesus in you and me.' Let us therefore make continuous efforts to be true representatives of him for all to see.

Scripture Verse

'Beware of false prophets, who come disguised as harmless sheep, but are really vicious wolves. You can identify them by their fruit; that is, by the way they act. Can you pick grapes from thorn bushes, or figs from thistles? A good tree produces good fruit, and a bad tree produces bad fruit. A good tree can't produce bad fruit, and a bad tree can't produce good fruit. So every tree that does not produce good fruit is chopped down and thrown into the fire. Yes, just as you can identify a tree by its fruit, so you may identify people by their actions.' (Matthew 7:15–20)

Reflection

What fruit are you producing as a representative of God's kingdom? Take a moment to audit yourself.

DAY 14

Critical Thinking and Decision Making

For those who are married, in a relationship, or simply have some knowledge of relationship dynamics, you may agree with me on the following statement: men and women are vastly different at making decisions.

Take my wife and I, for example. At times I just take a moment to marvel and smile at how the thinking and decision-making processes between us are so different. I'm the type of guy (and I believe that most men are this way) that when I go shopping, I have an idea of what I want to get. Therefore, my process is simple: I look for it, see it, and buy it. My wife ... well, let's just say that it's a production. Rest assured, though, that once she's made her decision, it turns out to be the one where she will get optimal satisfaction and benefit.

Having viewed her process of critical thinking and its impact on her ultimate decisions, I have come to learn and appreciate that this practice has value not only physically but spiritually.

When we fail to take time to critically think and analyse situations before we make a decision, we run the risk of coming to an end result that is detrimental to us. We must remember that we have an adversary

42

of our souls whose entire purpose is to steal, kill, and destroy. He is always looking for ways to ensnare and ultimately destroy us. We should never sacrifice long-term rewards for temporary satisfaction.

As we traverse this earth as kingdom citizens, we ought to be mindful through the Holy Spirit of the many ways the enemy will try to snuff us out. This requires us to think, and critically so, before we act and make decisions.

Our lives depend on it.

Scripture Verse

'Only simpletons believe everything they're told! The prudent carefully consider their steps. The wise are cautious and avoid danger; fools plunge ahead with reckless confidence' (Proverbs 14:15-16).

Reflection

Today, ask the Lord to give you the wisdom and discernment to avoid traps set by the enemy by rushing into decisions.

Section Three

TAKING SHAPE

In the same way, let your good deeds shine out for all to
see, so that everyone will praise your heavenly Father.
—Matthew 5:16

DAY 15

Putting it into Practice

When I entered university, I was eager and had high expectations, like most undergrads. I set a goal for myself, and everything I did during my tenure centred around this: graduating with first-class honours.

I knew achieving this goal would require the investment of hard work and focus. That hard work would include more than just studying but involve long days in the library, consistent attendance to lectures, and effective time-management.

Having the knowledge of what I needed to do to achieve the goal was step one, but step two and its many subcomponents would be even more crucial—*putting it into practice*. Without actually doing the actions that were required to succeed, I would not have been successful.

Similarly, as we read the Bible and attain a knowledge and understanding of God and his kingdom, we are required and expected by God to put his teachings into practice. Our lives ought to reflect the fruit of the Spirit and obedience to God's commandments. Doing this would mean being our brother's keeper, loving others as ourselves, exhibiting purity and humility, and doing the work of God.

Moreover, it is important to note that it will be in large part because of this component of practicing what we read that our heavenly

Father will be glorified and that the message of salvation and the gospel of Christ will spread throughout the world. Inasmuch as Jesus' words were impactful, so too was his ministry whilst here on earth supported by his actions.

> **As we continue to focus on what matters most, let us be encouraged to not merely be hearers of the Word, but doers!**

Scripture Verse

'But don't just listen to God's word. You must do what it says. Otherwise, you are only fooling yourselves. For if you listen to the word and don't obey, it is like glancing at your face in a mirror. You see yourself, walk away, and forget what you look like. But if you look carefully into the perfect law that sets you free, and if you do what it says and don't forget what you heard, then God will bless you for doing it' (James 1: 22–25).

Reflection

What teachings and commandments have you learnt from the bible that you have not been putting into practice? What are some tangible ways that you can start living out godly instruction?

DAY 16

One of the Greatest

P art of my tenure at university, as mentioned in an earlier devotion, saw me having the opportunity to study abroad for two years in the Bahamas. There, I attended a regional institution that had a mix of students from across the Caribbean. We all had our own unique cultures, but there was a definite overlap in similarities and interest. I soon found myself part of a friend group for both study and downtime. One particular Sunday, we were all feeling exhausted from the demands of student life to deal with the adulting realities of cooking, so we decided to take a nice leisurely walk down to the restaurant of choice: KFC.

When we arrived, we noticed a man dressed in heavily soiled and discoloured clothing standing by the entrance to the door with a stick in his hand. He tapped his stick asking for assistance with either food or money the moment we opened the door. After I analysed the situation, I noticed that this man was visually impaired, so once he heard the door open, it would have indicated that someone was either entering or exiting. Filled with compassion, I decided to purchase him a meal and a beverage.

What happened next would forever be etched in my mind. I gave him the meal, detailing what I had purchased. He took it gratefully, and as I turned to leave, he walked in the opposite direction. I watched to see where he was headed. At the end of the sidewalk, he sat beside another man, also clad in tattered garments. They began to share the meal.

I stared for a moment, in awe that even in this blind man's unfortunate circumstance, he was willing to share with another person in need. I also had feelings of regret, for had I known, I would have bought two meals! Fortunately, I saw both gentlemen a few months later at the same KFC location, and I was sure to bless them doubly.

In Mark 12:28-34, Jesus is once again being questioned by the religious leaders, many of whom were seeking to trap and later arrest him. Having been asked by one leader what is the most important commandment (vs 28), Jesus responded that it was to love the Lord with all your heart, mind, soul, and strength (vs 30). Without being further questioned, Jesus continued by stating that the second greatest is to 'love your neighbour as yourself', concluding that 'no other commandment is greater than these (vs 31).

I have come to learn that the act of giving is based on the concept of love. God is a big proponent of serving and giving, and all of it is predicated on his love for us. As we come into a deeper understanding of his love and also embrace it, God expects us to be walking examples of that love through our actions and interactions with others. When we do this, we fulfil one of the greatest commandments.

Today, as we love the Lord with all our being, let us also be sure to manifest this in our love and actions towards our fellow man.

Scripture Verse

'Jesus replied, "The most important commandment is this: 'Listen, O Israel! The Lord our God is the one and only Lord. And you must love the Lord your God with all your heart, all your soul, all your mind and all your strength.' The second is equally important: 'Love your neighbour as yourself. No other commandment is greater than these'"' (Mark 12:29–31).

Reflection

Share God's love today. Pick at least one way that you can show an act of love to someone you come into contact with today and follow through with it.

DAY 17

Making Wealth Common

On another occasion during the time I attended Bahamas Faith Ministries, the late Dr Myles Munroe spoke at great length on the concept of sharing wealth. This was a continuation of his teachings under the church's theme of kingdom citizenship and how the country of God operates.

To illustrate the point, Dr Myles gave the example of how we tend to hoard items we don't use. Oftentimes, these items could be utilized by others, especially those in need. He stated that this action of keeping things was contrary to God's governmental system, which is about sharing wealth. He cited this as one of the main reasons for global, widespread poverty. In God's kingdom, no one lacks. There is no classism, capitalism, or communism but rather *common* wealth.

To make this teaching practical, Dr Myles decided there and then that the church would engage in an activity to make wealth common throughout the assembly and local community. Congregants were asked to bring to church any item they no longer used but was in good condition that may be passed on to someone in need.

That following Sunday, the church and its exterior was filled with numerous items ranging from clothing to household appliances to shoes, to name a few. The stage was covered in various women's shoes.

The final count was well over one thousand pairs of all styles, sizes, and colours. The right corridor of the church had racks with hundreds of suits and other male clothing, while the left had similar numbers of female clothing and accessories. The car park had fridges, stoves, and even vehicles that people were no longer using!

The amazing thing about it all was this: all people who were in need of any item were able to access it at no cost. If you needed a fridge, it was free. You needed clothing? It was free. Food items, those were there too—and also free. This exercise showed what the kingdom of God is about: making wealth common for the benefit of all!

There is no better way to exhibit God's love than by sharing with those who may be in need. Living by this principle is truly a mark of a kingdom citizen.

Scripture Verses

'If someone has enough money to live well and sees a brother or sister in need but shows no compassion—how can God's love be in that person?' (1 John 3:17).

'The crowds asked, "What should we do?" John replied, "If you have two shirts, give one to the poor. If you have food, share it with those who are hungry"' (Luke 3:10–11).

Reflection

Aim today and going forward to use every opportunity you have, to share whenever there is someone in need. It does not have to be tangible. Even if it's just your time or spreading the gospel of the kingdom, it will go a long way.

DAY 18

Gratitude is a Must

Frequently, I find myself reminiscing, particularly on events and situations that occurred over various stages of my life. Memories of both great and challenging moments flood back to my mind in such detail, as if the events had occurred just a few weeks prior.

With all the changes in life that are occurring at a rapid pace, I count it a privilege to have the capacity to recall past experiences in detail (my wife often jokes that this is my superpower). Though recalling these experiences make for captivating storytelling and nostalgia, the theme that emanates is the faithfulness and goodness of the Lord. This is the common denominator across all my life experiences. There is just so much I have to thank him for.

Apart from my personal experiences, there is a story in Luke 17:11-19 that is a touching account of a man being moved by God's goodness and returning to express gratitude. Here, the account is given of when Jesus healed ten men afflicted by leprosy. Being labelled a leper was like being an outcast and led to banishment from society. Whilst Jesus was on his way to a village, these men, who obviously heard of his miraculous signs and wonders, saw him and sought to receive their healing. Like in previous cases, Jesus healed them and sent them on their way to be inspected by the priests, as was the custom in those times.

Upon recognizing that he was completely cleansed, one of the men made it a point to return to the Lord to give thanks and show his gratitude for his restoration. Acknowledging this man's act of gratitude, being the only one of the ten to return and give thanks, Jesus declared, 'Rise and go; your faith has made you well.'

The Bible does not give any further account as to that man's life after his experience with Jesus. However, it is clear that through this encounter, he understood just how good and faithful the Lord truly is. Based on Jesus' statement to him, Jesus noted how sincerely thankful this man was, and one can only surmise that he was doubly blessed for his act of gratitude.

In the moments we pause and reflect on our past, connecting the dots to realize how God has seen us through every success and every battle, let us be sure to show our thanks and gratitude to the Lord for his mercies, goodness, and faithfulness.

Scripture Verse

'Give thanks to the Lord, for he is good! His faithful love endures forever' (1 Chronicles 16:34).

Reflection

Pause for a quiet moment to express gratitude and thanks to the Lord for all that he has done for you, whether big or small. Count your blessings one by one.

DAY 19

Kick Doubt to the Kerb and Believe!

Back when I was 16, I had the distinct honour of being selected by my high school to attend the Global Youth Leaders Conference in Washington DC and New York City. After reviewing the details of the event and the full itinerary of activities, I realized this would be the experience of a lifetime, not to be missed! There was just one problem: attending was costly, and I knew my mother could not afford it.

Feeling the same way that I did about this exciting opportunity, my mother decided that we would pursue varying options in search of financial assistance and sponsorship. Unfortunately, as the date of the conference drew nigh, we had not received the responses and assistance that we were anticipating. Doubt set into my mind, and I later gave up on my prospects of attending.

God had a different idea. A few weeks later, I, along with a group of other young people from my country, was on my way to Washington and New York. A few sponsors reached out last minute, and all my costs were covered. I had a tremendous time!

In the days after my return, I recounted to my mother the many experiences that I enjoyed whilst on the trip. She smiled and beamed with satisfaction as she listened and viewed photos that I had taken. In our conversations, I admitted that I had doubts and had given up hope that I'd be able to attend. She then shared with me that God had audibly assured her one day as she was praying that everything would fall into place over the weeks leading up to the conference. She used this simple testimony and encounter to remind me that God has and always will supply our needs. He was true to his word. In the end, I really had no reason to doubt.

Luke 24:36–40 is one of the many accounts of Christ's appearance to the disciples after being resurrected. As with our innate and unbelieving human nature, those in attendance were skeptical to believe it was truly the risen Messiah and not a ghost. In an effort to sway the doubts of the disciples, Jesus revealed certain aspects of his physical self that ought to have changed the minds of his followers. He 'stood' (vs 36) and 'showed' (vs 40). He also encouraged them to 'touch' and 'see' and emphatically declared that it truly is him (vs 39). The disciples saw and believed after this.

Jesus is still in the business of making Himself known to us today in various facets of life. He feeds and clothes us, gives health, protects us, and provides for our every need. With this evidence, why then do we still have doubts? Why are we still troubled about what God has planned for our lives? Why, if we are truly living under the covering and guidance of the Holy Spirit, do we question God's plans for our future?

With all of the insurmountable evidence of God's faithfulness that surrounds us today, let us be confident in knowing that God is on our side and is true to his word.

Kick doubt to the kerb and believe. God's got us!

Scripture Verse

'One of the twelve disciples, Thomas (nicknamed the Twin), was not with the others when Jesus came. They told him, 'We have seen the Lord!' But he replied, 'I won't believe it unless I see the nail wounds in his hands, put my fingers into them, and place my hand into the wound in his side.' Eight days later the disciples were together again, and this time Thomas was with them. The doors were locked; but suddenly, as before, Jesus was standing among them. 'Peace be with you,' he said. Then he said to Thomas, 'Put your finger here, and look at my hands. Put your hand into the wound in my side. Don't be faithless any longer. 'Believe!' 'My Lord and my God!' Thomas exclaimed. Then Jesus told him, 'You believe because you have seen me. Blessed are those who me." (John 20:24-29)

Reflection

What are you believing God for today? Whether it is something tangible or a breakthrough, actively exercise your faith (by releasing any fear, anxiety or doubt) and wholeheartedly believe that God will act on your behalf and come through for you!

DAY 20

The Unconventional Lifestyle

The school I attended during my time in the Bahamas consisted mainly of nationals from across the Caribbean, including a few from the host country. Whilst there, I met a gentleman who later became my classmate in a financial management course we both took. He was many years my senior and was an established member of the local police force. He was seeking to explore other professional passions, which included working in the hospitality sector.

One day, he approached me and asked if I would be willing to privately tutor him, as he was having trouble in our accounts class. I obliged.

Whilst chatting at the conclusion of one of our study sessions, he said, 'Jay, I have a question. How come you don't carry yourself like the average 21-year-old? You don't behave or dress like them, and you seem to have different interests.'

I chuckled as I thought the question would have been related to the material we had just covered. I simply told him of the one factor that made (and still makes) all the difference in my life—Christ. 'My life is founded on my decision to live for Christ, so I strive every day to live like him and emulate characteristics of the kingdom.'

A detailed study of Jesus' ministry on earth showcases his unconventional lifestyle, which resulted in frequent opposition and challenge from the leaders of that time. However, in response to his opposition, he always made mention of his duty to represent his Father and the way of life in the kingdom of heaven. He taught and encouraged all to adopt this style of living, and he still does this today, through his word.

Living as kingdom citizens on earth sometimes may be met with opposition, bewilderment and outright disregard. There have been times due to my decision to follow the example of Christ that I was labelled as strange, boring, and even arrogant. We must remember, however, that the way we live should always represent Christ. Of equal importance is understanding that the way we live plays a critical role in sharing the gospel and the message of salvation to the world.

Living unconventionally may be unpopular, but maintaining a kingdom focus is key.

Scripture Verses

And so, dear brothers and sisters, I plead with you to give your bodies to God because of all he has done for you. Let them be a living and holy sacrifice—the kind he will find acceptable. This is truly the way to worship him. Don't copy the behaviour and customs of this world, but let God transform you into a new person by changing the way you think. Then you will learn to know God's will for you, which is good and pleasing and perfect. (Romans 12:1-2)

'And this is the way to have eternal life—to know you, the only true God, and Jesus Christ, the one you sent to earth' (John 17:3).

Reflection

Since giving your life to Christ and becoming a kingdom citizen, in what ways may you now appear peculiar to the world? Continuously pray that the Lord would strengthen you to daily follow Christ's example and emulate his way of living.

DAY 21

Family Ties

G rowing up, my late grandmother always impressed upon me the importance of maintaining the integrity of our family name. Back then, I thought that advice was her way of ensuring that I remained disciplined and not bring the name into disrepute. As I got older, I realized that one's name and its subsequent ties can have a large influence on the quality of life and experiences one may have.

World over, and in some societies more than others, a person's name brings with it a certain perception of what that individual's life will amount to. Wealth, access to a high quality of education, social status, and occupation are but a few aspects of life directly affected by the name one carries.

Here's a real-life example. A relative shared with me the story of telling the head of the company she worked for about my performance back when I sat the Common Entrance Exams (a very important exam for ten and eleven year olds in my native country for placement in secondary education institutions). When asked about my placement, my relative disclosed that I gained entry to one of my country's most prestigious high schools.

Then came the shocking response from the company head: 'Oh, I didn't know that Jason was of such material.'

My country's history dictates that placement at such a school was usually reserved for the elite of society. My alma mater was often limited to those with affluent family ties who were considered by society's standards as intellectually adept. Since I certainly had no such ties and came from a very simple background, it may only be deduced that I was perceived by that individual as not the "type" to attend such a school.

Little did he know, I am actually tied to a family whose name is above all names, and my inheritance is greater than can be imagined. I am a member of the family of God, and he calls me his own.

By accepting the gift of salvation given to man by God through his son Jesus, we are welcomed and adopted into the family of God. Having adopted his name, God gives us access to all that we need to live a life of victory, prosperity, and success in accordance with his perfect will. Therefore, we ought not to worry about the perceptions or the measurements the world uses to determine one's outlook for success and quality of life. We are not confined by these. As his children, the Lord's plans for us are always good and not for disaster but to give us a hope and a future (see Jeremiah 29:11)

In Christ, we have the opportunity to be reunited to the greatest family there is. There is no better family tie.

Jason O. Yearwood

Scripture Verse

'But to all who believed him and accepted him, he gave the right to become children of God. They are reborn—not with a physical birth resulting from human passion or plan, but a birth that comes from God' (John 1:12–13).

'God decided in advance to adopt us into his own family by bringing us to himself through Jesus Christ. This is what he wanted to do, and it gave him great pleasure' (Ephesians 1:5).

Reflection

What good news that you have been born again into the family of God! Ask Him to open your mind to the reality of the family and country that you belong to.

CONCLUSION:
THE BIG PICTURE

Contribution with a Purpose

The start of the decade saw the rapid spread of the COVID-19 virus throughout 2020. Eventually being declared a global pandemic, its impact brought many of the world's economic, political, and social activities to a screeching halt. The fallout from this adversely affected society's most vulnerable, who faced uncertainty regarding varying aspects of health and survival.

In the hardship brought on by the change and *threat* to life, the contribution of the brave and selfless helped with the provision of essential services to the wider populous and those most in need. These people pooled resources, skills, finances, and time to serve at this critical junction in history. From members of the health industry and civil service to charitable and private-sector organizations, there was tireless effort given to the cause.

The outbreak of the Covid-19 pandemic, tragedies, and rampant sin within our societies are signs of the times. For years we have heard that we are living in the 'last days.' Now more than ever, we are on the brink of this world-changing and eternal event—the imminent return of our Lord and Saviour Jesus Christ and the rapture of believers.

Just like the contribution made by those mentioned above, this devotional series was intended to contribute—from a spiritual perspective. A contribution to the advancement of the gospel of Christ, along with outlining how the principles of God and his kingdom may be implemented into our daily lives.

The sole purpose of this effort is to encourage you to accept Christ and keep him center in your heart and to actively live for and through him as a representative of his kingdom.

When we live as true representatives for God, his light will be sure to shine through us. This enables the sustained sharing of the good news that is the gospel of Christ, to always be shared in some form or fashion, with those who we come into contact with in our daily lives.

I pray that you have been blessed, encouraged, and equipped all for the glory and honour of Jesus Christ our Lord. Amen.

Scripture Verse

'And then he told them, "Go into all the world and preach the Good News to everyone"' (Mark 16:15).

We've done it! Congratulations to you on completing this spiritual journey on how God truly wants us to live as citizens of His kingdom even in this broken world system. Now that you have been enriched, I encourage you in like manner, to enrich those around you. Whether at school, home, workplace or at play, let's spread this wonderful news so that others may reap benefit and find peace in God and His kingdom. God bless you!

Printed in the United States
by Baker & Taylor Publisher Services